DSMS

A Kid's Guide to Drawing the Countries of the World™

How to Draw
Germany's
Sights and Symbols

Betsy Dru Tecco

The Rosen Publishing Group's
PowerKids Press™
New York

In loving memory of my father, Elwood Long, and to our German ancestors

Published in 2004 by The Rosen Publishing Group, Inc.
29 East 21st Street, New York, NY 10010

First Edition

Editor: Frances E. Ruffin
Book Design: Kim Sonsky
Layout Design: Mike Donnellan

Cover and inside illustrations by Mike Donnellan
Photo Credits: Cover and title page by Arlan Dean (hand); cover, p. 42 © Superstock, Inc.; pp. 5, 10, 36, 38 © Adam Woolfitt/CORBIS; p. 9 © Dallas and John Heaton/CORBIS; p. 12 © Hamburger Kunsthalle/bpk, Berlin; p. 13 courtesy Museum Oskar Reinhart Am Stadtgarten, Winterthur, Germany; p. 16 © Maurizio Lanini/CORBIS; p. 20 © Wolfgang Kaehler/CORBIS; p. 22 © Gianni Dagli Orti/CORBIS; p. 24 © Walter Sanders/Timepix; p. 26 © Vanni Archive/CORBIS; p. 28 © Paul Almasy/CORBIS; p. 30 © Lee Snider/CORBIS; p. 32 © José Fuste Raga/CORBIS; p. 34 © José F. Poblete/CORBIS; p. 40 © Hugh Rooney; Eye Ubiquitous/CORBIS.

Tecco, Betsy Dru.
How to draw Germany's sights and symbols / Betsy Dru Tecco.
    p. cm.— (A kid's guide to drawing the countries of the world)
Summary: Presents step-by-step directions for drawing the national flag, a castle, a stork, and other sights and symbols of Germany.
Includes bibliographical references and index.
  ISBN 0-8239-6685-2 (lib. bdg.)
1. Germany—In art—Juvenile literature. 2. Drawing—Technique—Juvenile literature. 3. Germany—Juvenile literature. [1. Germany—In art. 2. Drawing—Technique.] I. Title. II. Series.
  NC825.G48 T43 2004
  743'.83643—dc21
                                                                    2002013511

Manufactured in the United States of America

CONTENTS

Let's Draw Germany

You will find castles just about everywhere in Germany. Until the nineteenth century, the country was made of separate kingdoms, each with its own ruler. Every king had several castles. It wasn't until 1871 that a German prince named Otto von Bismarck brought Germany together as one nation. As Germany grew stronger, its army grew stronger, and Germany wanted more land. This desire for more land caused World War I in 1914. Germany and the countries of Austria-Hungary and Turkey, which were known as the Central Powers, fought the Allied Powers. The Allied Powers were France, Russia, Great Britain, Italy, and Belgium. In 1917, the United States joined the Allied Powers. By 1918, the Central Powers had lost the war.

After the war, a new government was set up. As the country's first democratic republic, it gave Germans the right to vote for their leaders. Instead of a king, a chancellor and a president were elected by the people. Then, in 1933, Adolf Hitler, leader of

Neuschwanstein Castle in Bavaria, Germany, resembles a castle in a fairy tale. It was built for King Ludwig II, and construction started in 1869. Much of the building of the castle had stopped by 1886, when Ludwig II was removed from the throne.

Germany's Nazi party, took over the country. He started the Third Reich, or empire. Hitler wanted this empire to grow, but his invasion of Poland led to the start of World War II. By 1939, countries of the Axis, or Germany, Japan, and Italy, were at war with the Allied Nations, or Great Britain, France, the United States, and the Soviet Union. Hitler even went to war against people in his own country. He had his army murder millions of people, both Jews and non-Jews, in several European countries.

Germany lost the war, which ended in 1945. Most of the country was destroyed. In 1949, it was divided into West Germany and East Germany. Each country had its own set of laws. Cities were rebuilt, and new industries were created. In 1990, Germany was again united. It has the world's fourth-wealthiest economy. This means Germany sells more products than any other country except the United States, Japan, and France.

Today the German government has a parliament with two houses, just as the United States has the Senate and the House of Representatives. A chancellor is the head of Germany's government.

Germany is a leader in education. In 1837,

Germany started the first kindergarten, a German word meaning "children's garden." It also started one of the first public school systems.

Now you can learn more about Germany. Once you read about some of Germany's most famous people and places, drawing them will be fun. You can follow step-by-step instructions that explain how to draw the subject in each chapter. Directions are under each step. New steps are shown in red. You will need the following supplies to draw Germany's sights and symbols:

- A sketch pad
- An eraser
- A number 2 pencil
- A pencil sharpener

These are some of the shapes and drawing terms you need to know to draw Germany's sights and symbols:

— Horizontal line

⬭ Oval

▭ Rectangle

▰ Shading

〰 Squiggle

⏢ Trapezoid

△ Triangle

| Vertical line

〜 Wavy line

More About Germany

Germany is about the size of Montana, at 137,735 square miles (356,732 sq km) though it has one-third the population of the United States. The total population is 83 million, and about 57 million people live in small towns and villages. The cities with the largest populations are Germany's capital Berlin, Hamburg, Munich, and Cologne.

The distant relatives of native Germans belonged to groups of people that settled more than 2,000 years ago in the different regions of Germany. Today more than seven million people living in Germany are from other parts of Europe and from Asia. The country's two major religions are Protestantism and Catholicism.

About one-third of Germany's workers have factory jobs. In fact, the country is one of the world's largest producers of manufactured goods. Germany makes some of the most luxurious cars in the world. Only Japan and the United States make more cars. As a leading steel producer, Germany makes steel for tools, machines, and ships. Many

This photograph shows the Kaiser-Wilhelm-Gedächtniskirche, built in 1895. Much of the church was ruined by bombs during World War II. A new church and a tall, modern bell tower were built in 1963.

chemicals for medicines are manufactured there. Fun things such as cameras and toys are also produced in Germany.

Most of Germany's small farms raise livestock and grow potatoes, and wheat and other grains. Germany buys many things, including different food items and fuel, from other countries.

Thanks to warm breezes in the winter and cool sea breezes in the summer, Germany's climate is generally mild. Temperatures near the coast stay above 30°F (-1°C) in the winter. Summer temperatures are around 70° F (20°C). Away from the coast of the North Sea, winters are colder and summers are hotter. The Alps get the most rain and snow. Germany's pleasant environment and strong economy promise a bright future for Germany.

This photograph shows the buildings on a small German farm near the town of Ulm in the region of Baden-Württemberg.

The Artist Caspar David Friedrich

The German painter Caspar David Friedrich once said, "The divine is everywhere, even in a grain of sand." He spent his career closely observing the mysteries of nature. He found a hidden meaning in everything from a rainbow to an old oak tree. Friedrich felt that true art is personal. It comes from the heart. It makes you feel an

Caspar David Friedrich

emotion and stirs your imagination. Artists who paint in the romantic style share this view. Friedrich was considered to be a romantic painter.

Friedrich was born on September 5, 1774, in Greifswald, Germany. He studied art at a school in Copenhagen, Denmark. However, he mostly taught himself to paint. Friedrich liked to paint landscapes of northern Germany. He was very interested in the Baltic Sea and its rocky coast. He thought the Harz Mountains were wonderful but scary. A firm believer in God and Christianity, Friedrich found a connection between nature and religion through his work.

Friedrich wanted to show that nature is bigger and more powerful than people. His painting entitled *Chalk Cliffs of Rügen* is a good example of this. It shows three people under tall trees. They look small compared to the very large white cliffs. In the distance, through the mist, is a wide sea. The painting's colors seem as cold as ice. The original painting is kept at the Oskar Reinhart Foundation Museum in Winterthur, Germany. Friedrich died on May 7, 1840, in Dresden, Germany.

Caspar David Friedrich created *Chalk Cliffs of Rügen*, an oil-on-canvas painting, in 1818–1819. Friedrich shows the power of nature in his painting. He painted the high, sharp cliffs of Rügen Island against the dark Baltic Sea. It measures 35"x 28" (90 cm x 71 cm).

Map of Germany

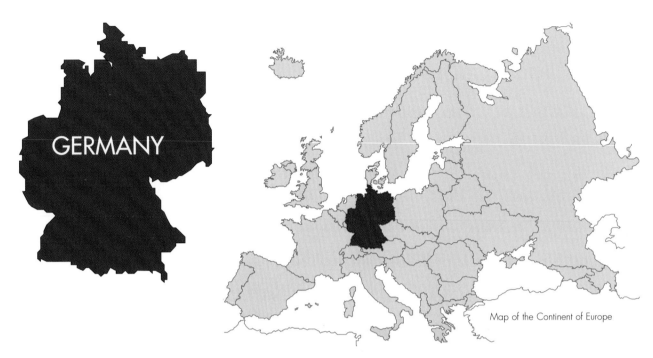

Map of the Continent of Europe

Germany is in the middle of Europe. It is bordered by the Baltic and North Seas, and by nine countries. Germany has five regions. The largest, the North German Plain, is low and almost flat. Germany's largest river, the Rhine, flows through it, as do other rivers. Rivers helped to shape the Central Highlands, a region of deep, rugged valleys and rocky plateaus. The South German Hills are lowlands that are ideal for farming. The famous Black Forest region is named for the dark fir and spruce trees that grow on its mountains. The Zugspitze, a mountain in the Bavarian Alps, is Germany's highest peak at 9,721 feet (2,963 m).

14

1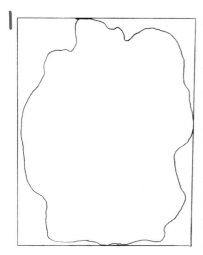
To draw the map of Germany, draw a large rectangle. Inside the rectangle, draw a wavy shape as a guide, as shown.

2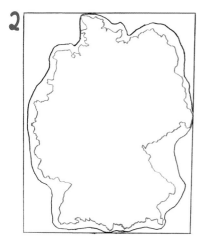
Within the guide shape, carefully draw the outline of Germany's borders.

3
Erase the rectangle and guide shape. Next draw a small star on the right to show where Berlin, the capital of Germany, is located.

4
To show the Rhine River, draw a long, wavy line from the middle left side of the map to the lower left. Draw a wavy line crossed by tiny lines to show the Danube River in southern Germany.

5
Next draw tree shapes on the left to show the Black Forest, and a triangle in the bottom center to show the Zugspitze.

6

⭐	Berlin
～～	Rhine River
┼┼┼┼	Danube River
△	Zugspitze
🌲🌲🌲🌲🌲	Black Forest

Next you can draw a map key to show Germany's special places.

Flag of Germany

Black, red, and gold are colors that were used by German rulers in the Middle Ages. Around the early nineteenth century, German troops wore black uniforms with red and gold decorations. The German flag's three stripes are also black, red, and gold. The tricolor flag has been used off and on at least three times. In 1949, after World War II, it was adopted for a final time. The official name of the German flag is Bundesflagge, or "federal flag."

German Euro

In January 2002, the European Union (EU) issued currency in the form of euro coins and paper money. Euros would be used in all of the EU's 12 member countries, including Germany. The front of the German 50-cent euro coin has 12 stars, for the EU's members, and the Brandenburg Gate, which is a symbol of both Germany's past division and its unity today. From 1945 to 1989, Germany was a divided country. The front of this euro also shows the date 2002.

Flag

1

Begin by drawing a large rectangle.

2

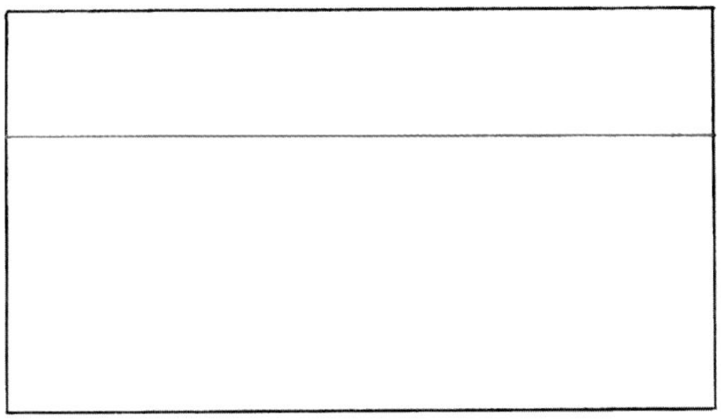

Draw a straight line one-third of the way from the top.

3

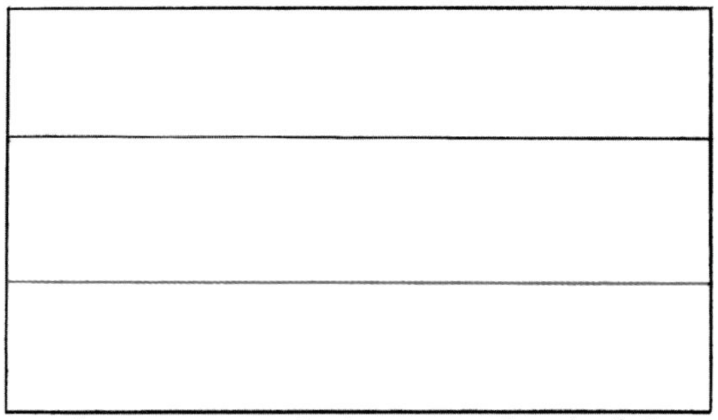

Next draw a straight line one-third of the way from the bottom.

4

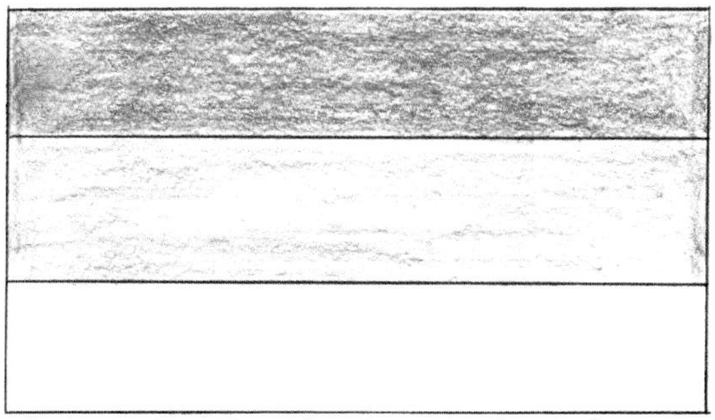

Finish your flag by shading in the colors as shown in the picture.

Euro

1

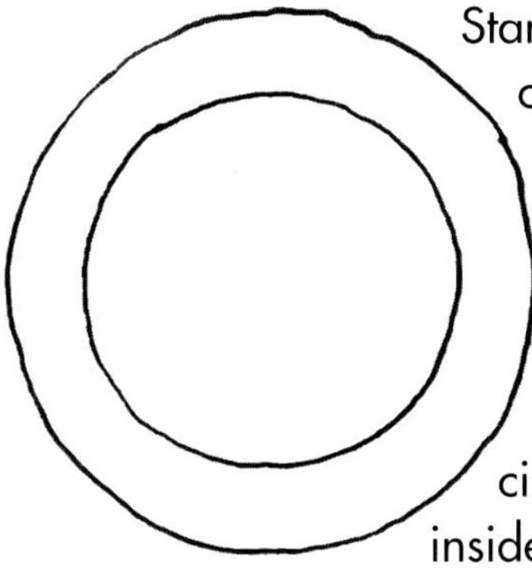

Start your drawing of the German euro by making a circle then by drawing another smaller circle on the inside.

2

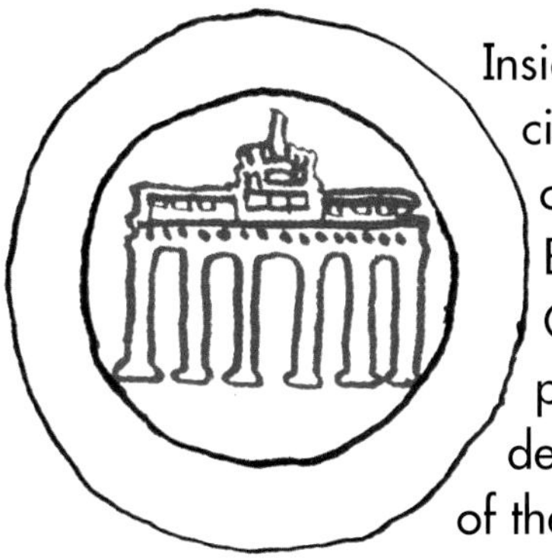

Inside the small circle draw the outline of the Brandenburg Gate with pillars. Add detail to the inside of the gate's top.

3

Continue to add the rest of the detail to the inner circle by drawing the lines at the bottom of the building and adding 2002.

4

Finish your drawing by adding the 12 stars around the outside of the inner circle and shading around both of the circles.

The White Stork

In Germany, it is not unusual to find a white stork sitting in her nest on the chimney of a house or on a church bell tower. These large birds make nests of sticks and stems that are big enough to hold a stork couple and up to five babies. Each spring, the male stork repairs the nest, and the storks use it again.

Storks are tall, graceful birds with long, slender necks. They grow about 3 feet (91.4 cm) tall. They are white with black flight feathers. Their feathers are wide and strong so that they can make the long flight each winter to Africa. White storks can run fast, but they usually move their long legs to walk slowly. One stork can eat about 100 insects per day. They also eat small animals, such as mice, frogs, fish, and worms. There are only about 3,000 storks left in Germany. The construction of new buildings has made it hard for storks to find good places to build their nests.

1

Start your stork drawing with a large, curved oval.

2

Draw another oval inside the first oval. Make small curves at the bottom for the stork's tail feathers.

3

Erase the first oval, then draw three lines, as shown, at the upper left side of the new oval to serve as a guide to drawing the head.

4

Inside this guide, draw an outline of the stork's head and beak.

5

Erase the guide around the head, and add a three-line shape to the bottom of the body. You will use this as a guide to drawing the stork's legs and feet.

6

Now draw the stork's legs and feet.

7

Erase the guide. Draw some wavy lines to show the top feathers of the stork's wing and the top of the leg. Draw an oval for an eye, and add tiny lines around the beak.

8

Shade the stork's head, back, and wings, and your drawing is complete.

19

The Cornflower

Germany does not have a national flower, but if it had one, the cornflower might be it. In fact, Kaiser Friedrich Wilhelm I, who ruled the German kingdom of Prussia from 1713 to 1740, chose the flower as a personal emblem, or crest.

Cornflowers grow wild in cornfields across Europe, including in Germany. They are also called bachelor's buttons because single men, or bachelors, sometimes wore the flower in their jacket's buttonhole. Cornflowers grow well in gardens, too. Many city dwellers in Germany own or rent small garden plots called *schrebergartens*, which are set up at the edge of town.

Cornflowers grow from 1 to 3 feet tall (30.5–91.4 cm). Their petals can vary in color from the popular blue to purple, white, or red.

1

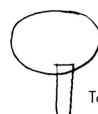

To begin your drawing of a cornflower, start by drawing a small oval. Add a long, thin rectangular shape. This will be a guide to draw the stem.

2

Inside the oval use squiggles to sketch an outline in the shape of a flower.

3

Erase the oval guide. Then draw long wavy lines in the stem guide.

4

Erase the guide rectangle, then add the wavy shape in the center of the flower.

5

Shade the cornflower and its stem as shown, and you're finished.

Charlemagne

The most famous ruler in Europe during the Middle Ages was Charlemagne, born Karl der Grosse. In 786, he became king of the Franks, a group of Germans who invaded Rome. By 800, Charlemagne's empire had grown so big that it included most of Europe. He wanted to spread the Christian religion. Pope Leo III, head of the Catholic Church, crowned Charlemagne emperor of the Holy Roman Empire. The pope might have wanted to make sure the king would continue to support and protect the church.

Charlemagne died in 814. He was buried in his palace chapel at Aachen, the German city where he lived. A cathedral, or church, was later added to the palace. It took 1,000 years to complete. Inside the cathedral is a bust, or statue, of this mighty ruler wearing a golden crown.

1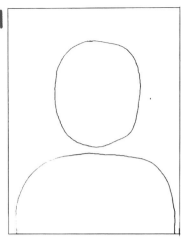
Start by drawing a guide rectangle. Then draw a circle in the center. Below it, draw a wide, upside-down *U* shape.

2
Erase the rectangle. Then draw a wavy outline of a face inside the circle. Next draw two short lines from the face to the *U* shape. Inside the *U* shape, begin the outlines of Charlemagne's shoulders.

3
After erasing the *U* shape, draw an outline of Charlemagne's hair and crown around the face.

4
Erase the guide circle around the head. Add details to the face. Draw ovals for the eyes. Draw the shape of his lips, nose, and mouth, as shown. Draw a curved line above the face for the base of the crown.

Begin the cross of the crown with a small rectangle.

5
Draw two curved lines from the nose to the hair to form the beard. Add another curved line above the crown, and fill in the space with small wavy lines. Draw an upside-down *U* for the center of the crown and then draw the outline of the cross. Add details to the neck, shoulders, and chest.

6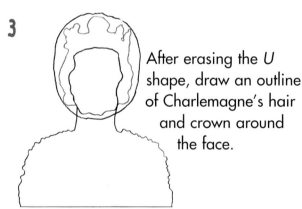
Draw small curved lines for the beard and hair. Add a circle at the center of the crown. Begin to draw the patterns on his chest and shoulders as shown.

7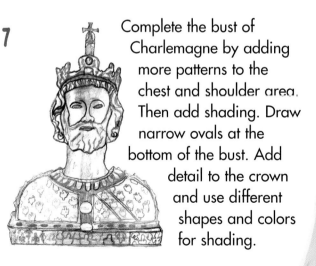
Complete the bust of Charlemagne by adding more patterns to the chest and shoulder area. Then add shading. Draw narrow ovals at the bottom of the bust. Add detail to the crown and use different shapes and colors for shading.

23

Bamberger Rider

Bamberg is a city on the Regnitz River in the Bavarian region of Germany. Before King Heinrich II became Holy Roman Emperor in 1014, he started to build a cathedral in Bamberg in 1004. This was to encourage Germans to become Christians. The great Bamberg Cathedral, as it looks today, took three centuries to build and to fill with monuments and art treasures. It is now considered to be one of the most beautiful German buildings from the Middle Ages.

Inside is the city's most famous sculpture, the *Bamberger Reiter*. Its name is German for "Bamberger Rider," and it shows a man riding his horse. Gothic sculptures such as this one were used mainly to decorate cathedrals and other religious buildings. Mystery surrounds the *Bamberger Reiter*. No one knows who carved this larger-than-life stone figure, or who the rider is supposed to be.

1 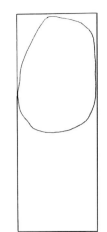 Start by drawing a large rectangle and an oval shape in the top half of the rectangle.

2 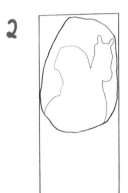 Inside the oval, begin to draw the shape of a horse's head and the top of the rider's body.

3 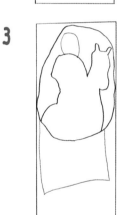 Continue by adding a round shape for the rider's head. Draw a guide for the horse's legs using straight lines.

4  Draw an outline of the head inside the round guide. Carefully draw the horse's four legs and feet inside the bottom guide.

5  Erase the large guide oval. Add the shape of the rider's arm and leg. Draw a square with rounded corners under the horse's feet. This will be the base of the statue.

6  Erase the guide. Add details to the rider's head. Draw a rectangle for the rider's face. Add lines for the hair. Draw a shape above and below the rider's arm. Use small ovals to draw the horse's eye and nose. Draw lines around the horse's neck and nose for the harness. Add the details to the base of the statue.

7  Draw small curved lines on the rider's body to show the clothing that he is wearing. Draw in details of the face. Draw the details of the horse's hair. Add more detail to the harness. Erase the square guide for the base. Then draw more small curved lines to the base to show that it was carved.

8  For the final step, shade the statue. Use shading to bring out the details of the sculpture's carvings.

Cologne Cathedral

Have you ever heard of a kind of perfume called cologne? The name comes from Cologne, one of the oldest cities in Germany. Germans pronounce it "*KOHLN.*" It is a key port along the Rhine River. During the Middle Ages, it also became a center of religion.

The symbol of the city is the Cologne Cathedral. It is the largest Gothic church in northern Europe. Construction began in 1248, but the cathedral was not completed for more than 600 years. The

building was hurt by Allied warplanes in 1944 during World War II. By 1956 it was fully repaired. As are most Gothic buildings, the Cologne Cathedral is incredibly big. It seems to reach into the clouds. Its twin towers, each rising 515 feet (157 m) high, were once the tallest humanmade structures in the world.

1

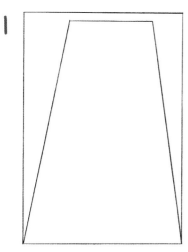

Begin with a rectangle and then add a trapezoidal guide shape inside to draw the two towers.

2

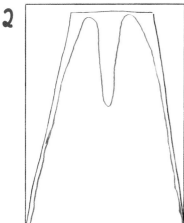

Next draw two rounded outlines to serve as guides for the cathedral's two towers.

3

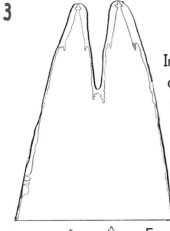

Inside the outline, draw the shape of the cathedral. Add a small cross atop each tower. Erase the rectangle and the inside guide.

4

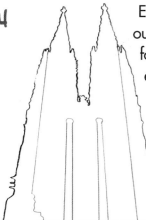

Erase the tower's guide outline. Add long shapes for the huge cathedral entrance. Draw straight lines on the left and right sides of the shape. Notice the squiggle on the left line.

5

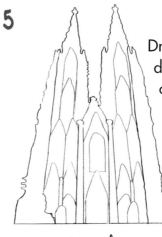

Draw the windows and different levels of the cathedral with several pointed shapes. Draw a large, pointed arch at the bottom of the cathedral.

6

Add V shapes and arches to bring out the details of the windows. Notice that the top windows have slightly different shapes than the lower windows.

7

Add curved and straight lines to bring out the detail of the structure. Add pointed shapes to show the series of windows near the top. Add a cross between the two towers.

8

Finish drawing the cathedral by shading it, as shown. Use different shadings, from dark to light, to bring out the depths of the windows and the towers.

Heidelberg Castle

Around 1400, Ruprecht III, a German ruler, started to build a splendid castle on a mountain above the town of Heidelberg. Heidelberg is a beautiful town in the Rhine valley. Only part of the castle stands today. More than 300 years went into building the entire castle. During that time, it was home to several noble families. The castle's many Renaissance buildings, tall towers, and famous gardens were once protected by four stone gates and a wall that surrounded a deep moat, or ditch. Between 1688 and 1693, French soldiers destroyed much of the castle and burned down the town. Lightning struck the castle in 1764, wrecking more of the structure. Today Heidelberg Castle is one of Europe's most ancient buildings.

1

To draw Heidelberg Castle, start with a long rectangle. Inside draw a long rectangle that has a step on the left side. Add a horizontal line on the right side.

2

Use these rectangles as guides to outline the tops of different parts of the castle.

3

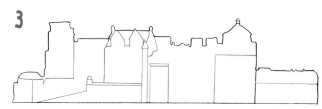

First erase the top of the guide rectangle. Then sketch in different sections of the castle. Use rectangles and straight diagonal lines.

4

Next add detail, including tiny shapes for the windows. Add short horizontal lines for ledges and vertical lines to add details.

5

Add more windows and then more straight lines for ledges near the top of the castle. Draw a tiny line above the tower at the far right.

6

To draw the trees that are in front of and around the sides of the castle, draw circles and shapes along the base of the castle. Add small rectangles for windows and other details, as shown.

7

Draw tiny lines to represent the bricks that make up the castle and the walls that surround it. Erase the bottom horizontal line.

8

Shade your drawing. The trees, the base, and some of the windows should have the darkest shading.

Gabled Houses of Bremen

Do you know the story of Hansel and Gretel? In the story, they are two children who find a house made of gingerbread and candy that's good enough to eat. The house in this German folktale, told by the Brothers Grimm, could have come from the gabled houses found in German towns such as Bremen. Bremen is a northern port city on the Weser River. At its center is a section called Altstadt, or "old town." Its narrow streets wind between rows of gabled houses dating from the fifteenth and sixteenth centuries. These richly decorated buildings, such as the Bremer Bank building in this photo, look like gingerbread houses straight out of a fairy tale. These gabled houses are made from wood and clay, not sweets. They are tall and attached to one another to make good use of a small space. The gables, or tops of the roofs, are shaped like steep steps. The shape helps rain and snow to slide off.

1 Draw a rectangle for a guide. Next draw a diagonal line near the top. Then draw two short lines at the left and the right, and two *L*-shaped lines at the right.

2 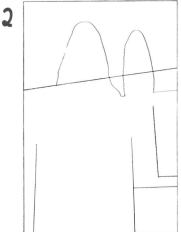 Begin to draw the gabled roofs of the structure with two large rounded peaks that cross through the diagonal line.

3 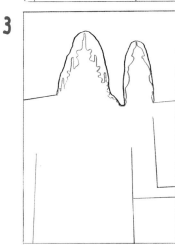 Erase the lines on the inside. Inside the peaks, draw curved spike designs that appear along the roof of the bank. The *L*-shaped and straight lines will be the columns of the bank.

4  Erase the top guides. Add details to the bank as shown. Notice the ledges and lines to show different sections of the building.

5 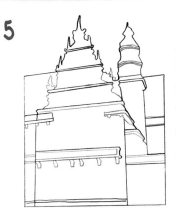 Add shapes to the ledges to show details. Starting from the top add all the lines shown in red.

6  For the bank's windows, draw rectangles, squares, and upside-down *U* shapes of different sizes. Draw a small shape near the top of the bank. Draw a small oval as a guide at the bottom.

7 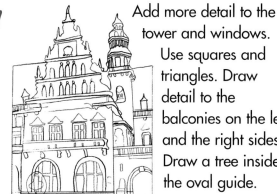 Add more detail to the tower and windows. Use squares and triangles. Draw detail to the balconies on the left and the right sides. Draw a tree inside the oval guide.

8  Add detail to the tree and erase the oval guide. Shade the insides of some windows and the tree. Finish your bank by writing "Bremer Bank" in the center.

The Brandenburg Gate

Today the Brandenburg Gate in Berlin stands as the symbol of a united Germany. Yet for about 30 years it was the symbol of a divided city. In 1961, a huge wall was put up to keep in people who wanted to seek freedom from East Berlin's communist government. When communism ended in Germany, the wall was torn down in 1990. Germans gathered at the Brandenburg Gate to celebrate the union of their city and country. The gate was built as an arch for King Friedrich Wilhelm II between 1788 and 1791. It measures 65 feet (19.8 m) high and 213 feet (64.9 m) wide. Above the stone columns is Quadriga, a bronze sculpture of a Greek goddess of victory and peace, driving a chariot, or a cart with four horses.

1

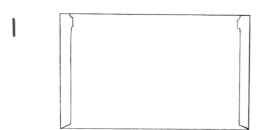

Let's start to draw the gate using a large rectangle for a guide. Next draw vertical lines at the left and right sides of the rectangle and add a slanted line going to each corner. These will be the sides of the Brandenburg Gate.

2

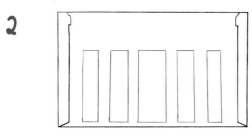

Inside the rectangle draw five smaller rectangles, as shown above. Make the center rectangle wider than the others.

3

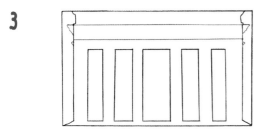

Next draw two horizontal lines just above the columns. Notice the small squiggle at each end.

4

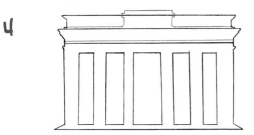

Draw horizontal lines above the ones you just drew. Add the shape in the center of the structure.

5

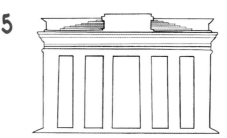

Draw small lines on each side of the small rectangle and long lines in the first ledge.

6

Draw a guide for the statue in the center. Add a rectangle and a line to the base. Outline small columns, and draw tiny ovals along the bottom ledge. Add details to the top ledge as shown.

7

Draw the statue in the center of the gate. Add a wavy line at the base of the statue.

8

Begin to shade the columns, the statue, and other parts of the gate. Darken the insides and the bottoms of the columns.

33

The Brothers Grimm

German fairy tales have been told by generations of people. Two German brothers, Jacob and Wilhelm Grimm, collected them from people all over Germany. In 1812, *Grimm's Fairy Tales* became the first collection of stories of its kind.

The Grimm brothers were born in Hanau, in the heart of Germany. They loved the stories told by their friends and neighbors. However, they worried that those stories and others would be lost. The Grimms went to work collecting and writing down 210 tales. As they retold the stories, they often made them more entertaining. Their fairy tales have been popular with people of all ages for almost 200 years. In honor of the brothers' work, the city of Hanau raised a statue of the Brothers Grimm, reading a book, of course!

1 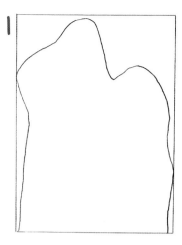 Start drawing the Grimm brothers statue with a large rectangle for a guide. Inside draw a guide shape for the two brothers in the statue.

2 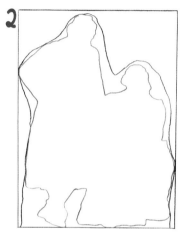 Inside the guide shape, draw the outline of the two figures.

3  Erase the outer rectangle and guide shape. Draw shapes to show a large book on the lap of one man and the spaces that outline the arms of the other.

4  Add detail to the two figures by sketching the outlines of their faces and arms. Draw detail on the clothing and a footrest, as shown.

5  Use ovals and straight lines, as shown, to draw the brothers' eyes, nose, and mouth. Add detail, such as long curved lines, for the wrinkles and folds in their clothing.

6  Continue to add more folds by giving the jackets even more detail.

7  Shade the statues. Notice that the folds in the jackets and the shadows around the faces are the darkest parts.

35

Carriage of Ludwig II

Ludwig II was born at Nymphenburg Castle in Munich in 1845. At the age of 19, he became king of Bavaria. However, Ludwig left others to rule the German kingdom while he built castles.

Ludwig was haunted by the desire to create more and more unbelievable castles. People thought he was so strange that they called him Mad King Ludwig. His most famous creation was Neuschwanstein Castle. A century later, it was the model for Sleeping Beauty's castle in Disney's Magic Kingdom theme parks. Ludwig II also had a large collection of sleds and carriages, or coaches. They were richly decorated and covered with gold. His carriages remain at the royal stables at Nymphenburg Castle.

This sculpture decorates the top of one of King Ludwig's golden carriages.

1

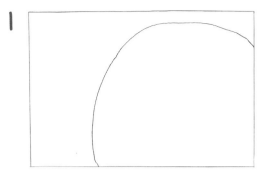

Begin the sculpture by drawing a rectangle for a guide and a rounded line inside of it.

2

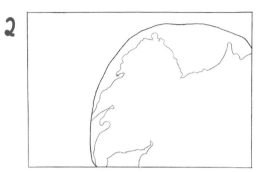

Inside the round line start the wavy outline of the statue.

3

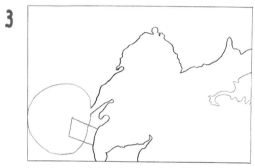

Erase the half circle. Add the shape on the right. Draw a small guide circle and rectangle on the left to begin a wreath and the statue's hand.

4

Draw an outline of the hand. Use small squiggly lines to draw the wreath.

5

Erase the guides for the hand and wreath. Draw a long curved line around the face to outline the hair. Add the eyes, nose, and mouth. Draw lines to show the gown.

6

Draw long, wavy lines to show the different strands of hair and the gown. Sketch in small wavy lines along the bottom right of the statue.

7

Add further detail to the hair and the wreath. Draw tiny crooked shapes to show the carvings in the bottom right of the statue.

8

Begin to shade the drawing. Make the folds of the gown and the base of the statue the darkest. Lightly shade around the face and the wreath.

37

Richard Wagner

Richard Wagner was born into a German family of opera singers and actresses in 1813. Wagner taught himself how to play the piano. He read Shakespeare's plays and studied the works of famous composers such as Beethoven. By the time he was 17, Wagner was composing music. During his life, he created operas, or musical plays. In Wagner's operas, performers show a wide range of emotions through the music. Love is a common theme in his works, which included *Tristan and Isolde*, *The Flying Dutchman*, and *The Ring of the Nibelungen*. King Ludwig II of Bavaria was a fan of Wagner's. With the king's help, Wagner produced many plays in Munich. Wagner died in 1883, at age 70, but composers continue to learn from his work. This bust, or statue, of Wagner is kept at Wagner's opera house, Festspielhaus, in a Bavarian town named Bayreuth.

1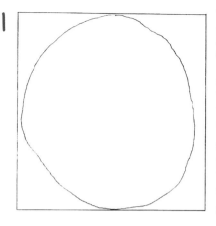

To draw the bust of Wagner, make a large rectangle for a guide. Next draw an uneven circle for a guide.

2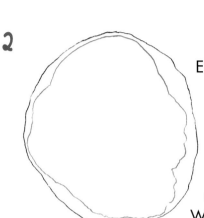

Erase the rectangle. On the inside of the circle guide, begin to draw the shape of Wagner's head.

3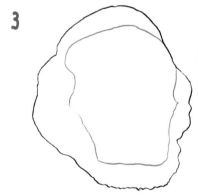

Erase the circle guide, and begin to draw the shape of his face.

4

Add a curved line at the bottom of the face to show the outline of his chin. Next draw almond shapes for his eyes. Add a turned-down line for the mouth. Use bent lines to draw his nose.

5

Draw lines for his pupils. Next add several curved lines to bring out the wrinkles in the face. Most of them will be around the eyes. Add another curved line to his lower lip and add a line for his upper lip. Add curved lines for more detail to the chin.

6

Draw lines to show Wagner's hair. For the beard draw many curved and wavy lines.

7

Begin shading the statue. The beard, wrinkles, and under his chin should be the darkest part of the shading.

39

The Reichstag

Just as the U.S. Congress meets in the Capitol building, Germany's parliament meets in the Reichstag. This is where the government makes the country's laws. The Reichstag was built in the center of Berlin, Germany's capital, between 1884 and 1894. In 1933, a mysterious fire destroyed much of the Reichstag. After repairs were made, it was hurt again during World War II in the 1945 Battle of Berlin. More repairs were made in the 1960s. The building got its new glass dome in 1999. Not all Germans approved of its modern dome. It is now a famous Berlin image. A sign on the building reads "Dem Deutschen Volke," meaning, "the German people." The Reichstag is a national symbol of unity.

1

Begin drawing the Reichstag with a long rectangle guide.

2

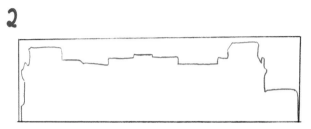

Next draw the outline of the top and sides of the building, as shown.

3

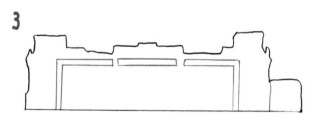

Erase the top of the guide rectangle. To show the different buildings of the Reichstag, draw two thick upside-down L shapes and a narrow rectangle in the center. Add a line at the right.

4

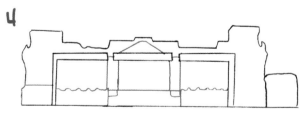

Add a triangle-shape with a flat top above the center rectangle. Next add straight lines to make three sections of the building. Then draw horizontal and wavy lines near the bottom of the building. Notice the small lines that connect the sections of the building.

5

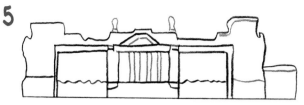

Draw a smaller flat-topped triangle shape inside the first. Add seven straight lines in the middle. Add lines for the details of the roofs of the building. Add round shapes as guides for statues.

6

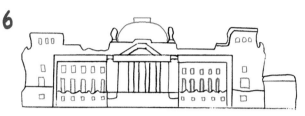

Draw squares and long rectangles to the drawing to show the Reichstag's many windows of different shapes and sizes. On the top draw a half circle and a rectangle for the dome.

7

Draw long horizontal lines for steps to the building. Add curved shapes to the left and right sections of the buildings. Add two straight lines on the roofs of the right and left sections of the building and other details. Add six lines on the dome. Draw the shape above the dome, which holds a light.

8

Shade the drawing, and you're finished.

The Messeturm

The second-tallest skyscraper in Europe is located in the city of Frankfurt. The Messeturm, or "trade fair tower," is a symbol of Germany's growing economy. Completed in 1990, the 842-foot-high (256.6-m-high) office building has 55 floors that are occupied by businesses. Its first floor is actually four stories high.

The Messeturm has a pyramid shape at the top that is 119 feet (36.3 m) high. Below the pyramid, the building becomes a glass circle. Below that, it is square shaped. A lot of concrete was used to build the Messeturm. For three days 240 workers poured 22,000 cubic yards (16,820.2 m³) of concrete from 90 trucks into a hole to make the foundation of the building. The hole was almost 20 feet (6.1 m) deep. The building has silver window frames and polished, rock columns made of red granite. At street level, in front of the tower, is an unusual sculpture called *Hammering Man*.

1

To draw the Messeturm skyscraper start with a rectangle and then draw two lines, one on the left and one on the right.

5

Draw curved lines across the top and then add parallel lines across the pointed top to show it is a triangle.

2

Using the lines as a guide draw the shape of the building's top. Note the pointed top.

6

Next draw a lot of straight lines. Draw them from top to bottom and from left to right.

3

Next draw in two sets of parallel lines on the left and right sides.

7

Draw squares and rectangles inside to show the building's windows.

4

Erase the outside guide and then draw the connecting straight lines at the top to show the many ledges.

8

Begin shading. Make sure the center is shaded the darkest.

Timeline

800	Charlemagne is named Holy Roman Emperor by the pope in Rome.
1517	Religious leader Martin Luther leads the Protestant Reformation in Germany against the Roman Catholic Church.
1618–48	The Thirty Years' War hurts Germany.
1871	Germany is politically united for the first time. A centralized government is formed.
1914–19	Germany starts World War I and loses, which ends the war.
1933	Adolf Hitler declares himself leader of the Third Reich.
1939–45	Germany starts World War II, then surrenders, ending WWII.
1949	The Federal Republic of Germany is formed in West Germany.
	The Democratic Republic of Germany is formed in East Germany.
1961	The Berlin Wall divides East Germany and West Germany.
1989	The East German government fails.
1990	The Berlin Wall comes down, and East Germany and West Germany unite.
1991	Berlin is chosen as the capital of the united Germany.
1999	The euro, the currency of the European Union, is introduced.

Germany Fact List

Official Name	Federal Republic of Germany
Area	137,846 square miles (357,019 sq km)
Continent	Europe
Population	82,386,000
Capital	Berlin
Most-Populated City	Berlin, population 3,392,900
Industries	Iron, steel, coal, machinery, vehicles
National Anthem	"Deutschland Lied" ("Germany Song")
Official Language	German
Common Phrase	*Guten Tag* ("hello" or "good day")
National Holiday	German Unification Day, October 3
Favorite Sport	Soccer, called football in Europe
Longest River	Rhine, 820 miles (1,319.7 km)
Major Lake	Lake Constance, 210 square miles (543.9 sq km)
Highest Peak	Zugspitze, 9,721 feet (2,963 m)
Major Religions	Protestantism, Catholicism
Boundaries	North Sea, Baltic Sea, Poland, Czech Republic, Austria, Switzerland, France, Belgium, the Netherlands, Denmark, and Luxembourg

Glossary

Allied Powers (A-lyd POW-erz) The countries of France, Russia, Great Britain, Italy, Belgium, and the United States during World War I.

Catholicism (ku-THAH-lih-sih-zum) The faith of Roman Catholic Christianity.

Central Powers (SEN-tral POW-erz) The countries of Germany, Austria, Hungary, and Turkey during World War II.

chancellor (CHAN-seh-ler) A leader of a group or a state.

Christianity (kris-chee-A-nih-tee) A religion based on the teachings of Jesus Christ and the Bible.

communist (KOM-yuh-nist) Belonging to a system in which all the land, houses, and factories belong to the government and are shared by everyone.

composers (com-POH-zerz) People who write and create music.

democratic (deh-muh-KRA-tik) Having to do with a government that is run by the people who live under it.

desire (dis-EYE-ir) Want.

divine (dih-VYN) Relating to God, or a god.

dome (DOHM) A type of curved roof.

European Union (yur-uh-PEE-in YOON-yun) A group of countries in Europe that work together to be friendly and to better their economies.

foundation (fown-DAY-shun) The part on which other parts are built.

gabled (GAY-buld) Roofs or tops of buildings that are shaped as steep triangles.

generations (jeh-nuh-RAY-shunz) People who are born in the same period.

Gothic (GAH-thik) A style of making buildings, popular from the twelfth to the early sixteenth century.

horizontal (hor-ih-ZON-til) Going from side to side.

industries (IN-dus-treez) Moneymaking businesses.

invasion (in-VAY-zhun) Attack.

Judaism (JOO-dee-ih-zum) The religion followed by Jews, based on the Old Testament of the Bible.

kaiser (KY-zer) The title for the rulers of Germany from 1871 to 1918.

landscapes (LAND-skayps) Pictures that show a view of natural scenery.

Middle Ages (MIH-dul AY-jez) The period in European history between ancient and modern times, from about A.D. 500 to about A.D. 1450.

Nazi (NOT-zee) Having to do with the German political party led by Adolf Hitler during World War II.

parliament (PAR-lih-mint) The lawmakers of a country.

plateaus (pla-TOHZ) Broad, flat, high pieces of land.

Protestantism (PRAH-tes-ten-tih-zum) A religion based on Christian faiths.

pyramid (PEER-uh-mid) A large, stone structure with a square bottom and triangular sides that meet at a point on top.

Renaissance (REH-nuh-sons) The period in Europe that began in Italy in the fourteenth century and lasted into the seventeenth century, during which art and learning flourished.

representatives (reh-prih-ZEN-tuh-tivz) People chosen to speak for others.

republic (re-PUB-lik) A form of government in which the people elect representatives who run the government.

romantic (roh-MAN-tik) Having to do with an art form, begun in the eighteenth century.

Soviet Union (SOH-vee-yet YOON-yun) A former country that reached across Eastern Europe and Asia to the Pacific Ocean.

stables (STAY-bulz) The buildings in which horses are sheltered and fed.

symbols (SIM-bulz) Objects or designs that stand for something else.

united (yoo-NY-ted) Brought together to act as a single group.

vertical (VER-tih-kul) In an up-and-down direction.

World War I (WURLD WOR WUN) A war fought between the Allies and the Central Powers from 1914 to 1918.

World War II (WURLD WOR TOO) A war fought Great Britain, France, Russia, and the United States against Germany, Japan, and Italy from 1939 to 1945.

Index

Web Sites

Due to the changing nature of Internet links, PowerKids Press has developed an online list of Web sites related to the subject of this book. This site is updated regularly. Please use this link to access the list:
www.powerkidslinks.com/kgdc/germany/